Soul Songs

by
Dorsey Taylor

MGB Publications

First Edition 2020

SOUL SONGS

MGB Publications

ISBN: 978-0-578-74848-1

Cover design by Jacques Bouvard.

Many thanks to Milt Reilly for his endless help.

TABLE OF CONTENTS

INTRODUCTION

Dorsey Taylor is an unusual prisoner. He is a musician, a composer and writes poems and short stories. He makes the other inmates happy with his music and brings a smile to their faces. And he is deeply religions. Most of all, he shows us that although there are walls around him, inside him he has a vast world of love, faith and music that no walls can take away. Also, even though he is a devout Christian, he celebrates every religion in his writing. The famous Chinese world renowned painter Ai Wei Wei wrote, "Art is about aesthetics, about morals, about our belief in humanity. Without that there is simply no art." [1]

He is dealing with diabetes, a mental health problem, and was once alcoholic, which is an illness not a vice. While in prison he has received certificates of accomplishments: from Alcoholic Anonymous celebrating sobriety, a certificate of achievement for participating in the Mental Health Recovery Seminar, a Professional Development Certificate for Successfully completing the Center for People in Need TRADE program, Life Skills Workshop, and a Certificate of Completion in Effective Communication and Conflict Resolution Workshop. He has also managed to lose a lot of weight which is helpful for diabetics.

Although he had a very difficult childhood and lived in places where there was danger, and witnessed the good friends of his brothers being shot to death, blood on the floor, the sounds of ambulances and of guns, he also had love in his family. His mother worked the night shift as a nurse and Dorsey loved his

---

[1] Humanity. Ai WeiWei. Edited by Larry Walsh. (Princeton University Press, 2018) pp.21.

parents. His older brothers and their friends were with him very often when he was only eight years old, but one of them died in a car accident during the winter. In short he lived a life that is often hidden from people who are well off, but which is dangerous and where children are very much at risk. Intertwined with this is the fact that many of his brothers' friends were musicians known from coast to coast and many of their friends served in Vietnam, so there is often an intertwining of joy and sorrow, the sorrow helping us understand joy. Anyone who reads the Jesuit Priest Gregory Boyle's book, "Barking to the Choir," will find out about healing in the long term, and how so many youngsters he helped over the years went from experiencing trauma to having very good lives.

There have been nationwide protests across the country against the killing of black people by the police. This time they are very diverse and the majority of the country supports them. But that did not help Dorsey Taylor who was arrested for stealing. His lawyer argued that given his mental illness he should not be incarcerated because he could not receive the proper care. But the judge claimed that he could possibly be a menace until the end, and decades later, Dorsey is still in prison with no chance of release despite his exceptionally good behavior. The judge's ruling's has layers of meaning, i.e. that Dorsey is not a good person. He is suffering from what I can only refer to as imposed guilt resulting from his long sentence. Yet though his suffering has been defined by racism, his poems also reveal his understanding that we need to celebrate diversity, not just in religion, but in the Creator's rainbow of colors.

Dorsey Taylor shows us what many people do not realize, that living is a constant learning experience, that he has grown in many ways and accomplished so much behind walls. His favorite book is the bible which he often quotes. He is now able to write in Italian, French and Spanish. This is an important lesson to all of us who may have a narrow view of success, a life well lived despite the cruelty and injustice he is living with.

Dr. Marguerite G. Bouvard

DEFY SONG

Either defy or fail.
You'll defy da odds,
start your own business
or get a better job
after time in jail.
Know I just couldn't fail
or let pessimism win, again.
Had to somehow overcome
mental illness-so
I put negativity on the run.
Get or got rebuilt into
the 20 million dollar
man or woman
therapy for the mind,
holy positive mind
water turned into wine.
For spirit for those
who wanna hear it.
Exercise and relaxation
for body no longer a jerk.
But after all de hard work,
vacation time cause,
success is mine; and I find
what I was looking for..
I had all da time!
Just needed a lil help.
mentor and stop program
"DEFY'

AA AND OTHER NAY SAYERS

If you want small talk
before meetings AA any day,
they say he only came for
the coffee, kool-aid or tea.
Ended up getting a key
to 'nlock' 'nhibitions and a new destiny.
Now there're free cause
through the conversation,
which was transportation,
went through a total transformation
which led to a more positive destination.
And now he can see clearly
how to walk in victory.
All past troubles are history.
Made new friends, remember
saying at the end, keep coming back.
If it's free with knowledge
got it made in the shade.
The poem is for those
who talk about others;
mother, father, sister or brother.
"For whoever does the will of
My father is in heaven,
My brother and sister
and mother." (Matt 12:50).
"For I was hungry and you gave me no food.
I was thirsty and you gave me no
drink." (Matt 25:42)
"then he will answer them saying,
Truly I say to you, as you did not do it

to the least of these, you did not do it
to me." (Matt 25:45).

FATHER'S DAY POEM

You never said I'm leaving
You never said goodbye,
and only God knew why.
A million times I needed you,
A million times I cried.
If love alone could have saved you
you never would have died.
In life I loved you dearly.
In death I love you still.
In my heart you hold a place
that no one could ever fill.
It broke my heart to love you,
but you didn't go alone,
for part of me went with you,
the day God took you home.

FUNERAL POEM

for Denise Ladd

Best friend I ever had, I'm sad,
but she is glad. Denise is now at peace.
Yeah, she moved on to claim
her other throne, queen all her life,
She did it right. She lived her dreams.
I saw no wrong. She showed no fear.
She's now singing songs of joy.
No more tears. The real deal. Ms. Mcoy.
Her choir of angels are singing. All ears
should be ringing, when we think about
her voice, and that most beautiful smile.
It was always her choice, to complement
you on your style, always positive
and willing to give, so the less fortunate
would live hearts of gold. She was the most
beautiful soul, a platonic friend who would have
you back to the very end. Now, no more
pain, everything's new, body, mind, even
shoes. Now she's walking on top of da
rainbow, no more blues.

2

Denise, be at peace, it's the end of phase
one. Now you are into phase two.
You left a son, sad and blue, friends
and men who wanted your attention.
Now they don't know what to do, but

put you in suspension and deal wit da
real, and let you live on in memory.
Your beauty made men stammer.
She was not my siria dama,
but a mama jama, soft spoken,
always open for conversation.
Travel in peace, to your next
destination. Take no quilt. You did
your best. You are now part of a quilt
cover and rest. Big respect, no more
rat race. Jesus got you through grace.
Your case, "guilty of being for rest,
no penalty. But a reward for living
in da good Lord." Wear your crown
Queen. Get down, heaven, earth, church.
Revelations 21.4. He will wipe away every tear
from their eyes, and death shall be no more.
Neither shall there be mourning, nor crying,
nor pain anymore. For the former, things have
passed away. 5. And he who was seated on
the throne said: "Behold I am making all things
new." Also he said, "Write this down, for those words
are trustworthy and true." 6. And he said to me,
"This is done. I am the alpha and omega, the beginning
and the end. To the thirsty I shall give from the spring
of the water of life without payment." 7-31-18-88-1-18.

GUILTY CONSCIENCE

A guilty conscience will never let you be free,,
till you get 'n your knees, confess and give your testimony.
It'll stop you from hearing voices,
seeing shadows, making bad choices,
and not crossing your fellow man.
"Just so you understand, that what you do
to the least of one of these, you do to me."
Then they were answering him saying,
"When did we see you hungry or thirsty,
or a stranger, or naked, or sick,
or in prison and did not minister to you?
And these will go away into eternal punishment
but the righteous into eternal life."

So folks should think twice,
'fo you go into a wicked conspiracy,
to cut the rope of the brother who gave your hope.
We all make our own shadows in life,
wrong or right, either in darkness or in light.
We row our boats to either shore,
reach our destination night or day
and what else does scripture say?

"And you will know the truth,
and the truth will set you free."
So if the Son sets you free
you will be free indeed.
For whoever does the will of my Father in heaven
is my brother and sister and mother.
So, will you cut the rope of your own brother,

make your mother cry? I guess Cain did Abel.
Judas went insane. Cain will never be stable.

Wake up, have to get 'high,
then wonder why, mother's cry
and storm, out of the norm
cause they're operating and
motivated by hate and jealousy.
Conscience is guilty!

Now, Jesus comes to set the captives free.
Don't be like the hopeless sinners in history.
Carry the Good Book and talk the talk
not knowing folks are watching your walk.
Games against God will drive you away.

A GHETTO CURE THAT WORKED

Went back to my inner church. Rhymes for da mind, true for me. You?

Never knew bout psychiatry. In the early sixties and seventies, it was in church giving testimony. And if that didn't work to cure your ills, more prayer was added to

help you over the hill. Anyway you couldn't break da code and talk to da man, even if he wanted to lend a hand. There was a road we felt well traveled by many,

but only we could identify. So what some didn't get into religion, how on faith got superstition. And we all know the two don't mix, da proper fix. Oh the other temporary artificial

simulation- satisfaction. So if there wasn't enough food, clothes, shoes, no TV, no action, back to da stress, just so you and your family can eat.

where you might choose to wear any number of hats, all the while suffering from PTSD. One day the mack, next day pool shark, all around player and hustler,

didn't matter which show long as you came home wit da dough. So, dis is da norm. In almost every hood, trying to follow your dream, but end up being Bro, B. good.

Then, cause of miracles and values, you wrestle at night, toss and turn till daylight, wake up, na cold sweat, not time for regrets, cause you got to keep on, keeping on, an you not all bad, cause every Wednesday and Sunday, you go to church, ask for forgiveness, thank da good Lord, for letting you see another day. And now its

depression, PTSD, and multiple personalities. Years ago God stepped in, tried to protect your prayers, be savior and friend, no other available remedy. You wouldn't listen

cause your stomach was touching your back and it's hard for a kid to stay on track, stomach inspiring mind to make da wrong music and it motivating his

make sandwich,

open cookie box. Start of another day. Lunch. For breakfast, never heard of bacon and eggs. But you're on your way. Got to get some money. Always dress for success.

In and out of places with a crew of two or three night time. Eat and drink a lil wine. Than age 12, that week, few prayers were answered and in a truck van full

of candy looking for boys club. Fate or good luck. Everybody in that hood and others could use a paying job. Then they wouldn't have to steal or rob. So after school

I put em all to work. We made lots of money. For every box of candy we sold we kept 20-25 percent. It's cool, milk and honey. Now what's funny got on my snakes,

gater, lil strassi pin stripped sansa belts. I really believe Jesus wept. Felt like I was chosen to be one of his reps, but kept being pulled out of step.

IN THE DISTRICT COURT OF THE PEOPLE

PEOPLE

VS

SELF PROCLAIMED MESSANGER

WHO TALKS TO GOD AND MADE

CONNECTIONS TO THE TRINITY

REQUEST FOR

INDICTMENT,

ALLEGATIONS ASSERTS

TRUE

DEMONSTRATION OF REAL

FAITH, HEALING,

FORGIVENESS,

POSITIVENESS AND TOTAL

TRANSFORMATIONS

CHARGES! THEN COUNTS!

WE, THE PEOPLE, SAY THIS MAN HAS BEEN RAISING PEOPLE'S EXPECTATIONS. TALKING BOUT, HEAVEN IS FREE. JUST ELEVATE THROUGH THE TRANSFORMATION, BATHE IN THE SALVATION, BY JUST WATCHING, TASTING THE FRUIT THAT FALLS FROM HIS TREE. YOU TOO

CAN CLAIM VICTORY. WE SAY THIS IS BLASHPHEMY, AND WE WANT TO SEE HIM TURN WATER INTO WINE, THAT MIGHT JUST SATISFY OUR MINDS.

CT.1. BEING TOO COOL, CAPTIVATING SOULS USING SPIRITUAL TOOLS.

FROM GOD'S SCHOOL OF LOVE. ULTERIOR MOTIVE, REMOVE INFERIOR ABORTIVE THOUGHTS, REPLACE WITH SUPERIOR, REEL IN THE LOST.

SHOW "'EM" HOW TO GET DOWN, ONCE THEY'VE FOUND, TRUE SELF, COUNT 2. CHARGE OF HAVING BIG, JUICY, FRESH RIPE FRUIT FALL FROM

HIS TREE. IT PROVIDED LIGHT IN THE DARKNESS, HUMOR, HEALED, LIFTED BURDENS, GAVE BELIEVERS A REAL TESTIMONY.

COUNT 3. HE CAREFULLY AND FULLY EXPLAINED GRACE, DEMONSTRATING THE WORKINGS OF, EVIDENCE OF FAITH, ENCOURAGING BELIEVERS

NOT TO RACE, SHOWING ALL INTERESTED HOW TO GIVE THEIR CARES OVER IN PRAYER, PROMOTING POSITIVITY AFTER EXPERIENCING

CLARITY POINTING TO THE RIGHT ROAD TO VICTORY.

COUNT 4. JUDGES SAY ! WE LIKELY GOT TO IGNORE. CAUSE HE DID THIS FOR MEN AND WOMEN, ON PHONES, IN THE MAIL AND FOR CHILDREN TOO. NO ONE WHO ASKED WAS EXCLUDED FROM AN HONEST ATTEMPT OR GOOD ADVICE, FOR THE BETTERMENT OF LIFE. DOES NOT MATTER BOUT COLOR. HE'S COLOR BLIND, SEES ALL AS SISTERS AND BROTHERS IN CHRIST IF THEY SIMPLY WANNA CHANGE YOUR LIFE FOR THE BETTER, JUST CALL OR WRITE A LETTER.

JUDGES ! WE SIMPLY CANNOT FIND THAT HE'S DOING ANYTHING WRONG. HE EVEN PUT IT IN MUSICAL SONGS, FOR THOSE WHO WANNA DANCE, HE FULLY EXPLAINS THE SECOND CHANCE, OR AS SCRIPTURE SAYS. HOW MANY TMES SHALL I FORGIVE MY BROTHER/ HOW MANY TIMES WILL TWO PEOPLE GO TO THE SAME TREATMENT CENTER FOR DRUGS. SAME METHOD, ONE PERSON, IT MAY ONLY TAKE ONCE, THE OTHER MAY TAKE AS MANY TIMES AS IS NECESSARY, OR UNTIL THEY GET READY. PEOPLE GET READY, THERE'S A TRAIN COMING, DON'T NEED NO TICKET, JUST THANK THE LORD.

VERDICT ! AND ORDER!

GOSPEL INDICTMENT SERIES CREATED BY DORESEY TAYLOR SR.

FOR EDUCATIONAL AND ENTERTAINMENT PURPOSES. ORIGINALLY BEGAN AFTER THE 'LOVE INICTMENTS' IN 1997 CONTINUED IN 2001, AND BEFORE THAT THE YEAR 1977. REVISED 1978. CONTINUING MUSICAL, PLAYS, LYRICS

IN THE EARTHLY COURT OF HEALING PETITION OF PLEAS

FOR ONE WHO'S SYMPATHETIC

TO DIABETICS

REQUEST TO AN EARTH ANGEL

FROM A CHANGED MAN, WHO

NOW UNDERSTANDS

PLEASE, I'D LIKE TO THANK YOU FOR BEING INSTRUMENTAL IN HELPING ME RESTORE WELLNESS AND FREEDOM. NOW ONCE AGAIN I'M

FREE TO GO ON AND SPREAD THE NEWS SO OTHER DIABETICS CAN NURSE THE BLUES.

IT WAS UP TO YOU TO ACESS A PENALTY, AFTER MY CONFESSION ON INFRINGEMENT. I FEEL GOD REALLY DID BLESS, BY GIVING ME A THERAPUTIC TESTIMONY SO ON INSULIN I'M NO LONGER DEPENDENT.

I'M A LIBERATED SURVIVOR NO LONGER A MEDICATED DENIER. BUT NOW WALK AND RIDE THE ROADS AND STREETS WITH PRIDE, PATHWAY THROUGH MY SPIRIT AND SOUL, SAYS, BE OF GOOD CHEER, DO NOT HIDE WHAT'S INSIDE, OF ALL WHO MIGHT'VE

FEEL, OR GOTTEN SICK, THEY GOT TO SIP FROM THE WELL. IT'S NO TRICK WHEN THEY GET WELL, THEIR DOCTORS WILL WONDER HOW THEY BROKE THE SPELL. TELL 'EM HOW YOU TOOK POTION FROM A BOOK, THEN AFTER A SECOND OR THIRD LOOK, YOU FELT THE NOTION. THAT'S ALL IT TOOK. SO, IF SHE AGREES, CLAIM SUCCESS WITH GOLDEN KEYS, SWEAR GOD DID BLESS, AND YOU, HE'LL USE TO SPREAD GOOD NEWS, TO ALL THE REST.

VERDICT; GUILTY OF USING A SPECIAL FORUMLA, OR POTION, BUT AS TO HIS MOTION, GRANTED, PENALTY, SPREAD TRUTH AND JOY AROUND THE WORLD TO EVERY DIABETIC MAN, WOMEN, BOY AND GIRL.

IN WITNESS THEREOF, I HAVE ACKNOWLEDGED AND SIGNED THIS DOCUMENT. DATED THIRD DAY OF JUNE, 2016.

PRELUDE TO LA BELLA CONSCIENTE DEL PACIFICO

La bella Donna da Rella, There is no such thing as a food called real love, maybe filet mignon, steaks, caviar, ribs, BBQ, brisket, father bones, rib eye, specialty pie can give you a Jones. It only exists in dreams and fantasies, what artificial hearts are made of; knights, queens, duals, sword fights, cold and hot sweats fuel da nights. Why bother, water in a desert oasis, beautiful faces vanish without a trace. Then deny every time and swear it's not a crime. Who really cares, or does time, heartaches make love disappear like vapor, then gritty swear, it's not a caper, gotta follow the paper trail, to capture da quail, never fails, hunter, huntress, gun, trap, fish bait love or hate. If it looks sweet, do you first greet then eat. Will personalities meet, agree in peace?

SONG WITH A JAMAICAN ACCENT

Be forgiving mon pti I tell ye bloke my heart
       ye made me cry, me be forgiving
stead of saying bye bye.
       me was so hurt me wanted to die
but it say in God's work give it another try
       me be forgiving mon, me be forgiving
Don't care if you Rasta man, Muslim or Jew
       the word in every language speaks to you.
It say be forgiven mon, be forgiven.
       The love that we had was of so good.
But your intentions were no earthly good.
       You put a mo-jo on me to steal
me soul. Sent me min on a blind lover's stroll.
       Maybe me was loco for falling for the
mo jo. Like a hoss lead to water, me had to
       take a drink. You stirred up me emotions, left
me unable to tink. Me be forgiven mon. Me
       be forgiven.

SOUL TALK 5

      Soul talk 5 is to inspire all, to keep hope alive,
of what side of da tracks you came up on. Was it wrong if
      you had to take dope, just to cope, or wine to relax
a troubled mind. For fears or everyday stresses, whether
      there was a shrink available or not, and you didn't think, relighting up
dat pot. This is bout breaking addictions,
      letting go of de superstitions, going through da
stop sign. In your mind getting on with life, no more rolling
 dice. But taking two slices
   from da cake of life called paradise. Discovering your
creativity, marching on, in music and song, to victory. Da good book
   says. Don't be misled. Mathew 7-4, for the gate is narrow
and the way is hard that leads to life, and those who find it are
   few. After many ups and downs, peace, real love, victory. Success
can be found. We all come to cross dat crossroad where higher spirit
   inspires soul, or fewer desires dominate control. And from this point on
it should be a different song. After da burn, you got to say
   you learned, in and out of psych wards and jails, trying hard to turn invisible
cards, never again wanting to be in hell or to admit you failed. Walk along
   to your own groove. Don't let nobody steal your cool, wit loud voices, poison
darts, words, not of choice
      which will come out like steel and hurt so bad,
   it'll steal your worth, reduce you to the size of an ant. There is no such word as
can't. Now I know this song is kind
      of long. But I had to get my point
   across without smoking a joint. So you don't get lost. Soul talks, ain't no jive.
Give your spiritual brothers, and sisters a high 5. Help to keep hope alive.

SPIRITUAL HEALING; ORLANDO, VEGAS, WORLD SURVIVORS, VICTIMS, SOUL SPEAKS ENOUGH !

Here is the dark, tall mountain the world needs to leave
       behind. News every day speaks of another heinous,
bizarre crime. So I know this mountain's view is not only
       just in my mind. Seems years ago in another space
and time, we all for equal rights, we all had to fight, color didn't matter
       because in the Creator's eyes, we were all sisters and brothers, wanna
break it down a little clearer
for the narrow minded who didn't
       find it, Red, yellow, black, white or brown, you either grow physically
into a man or a woman, and as you evolve spiritually, you should influence
others
       positively, to grow from within and show 'em how
to remove obstacles, grab the impossible. It's no mystery.
All throughout history, it's been done time
       and time again. Try to be a light in da dark, do it right, illuminate the
whole pack and if you're doing it, you can. In others you should see no wrong,
But leave it to the ultimate match maker, he's the one who put the two halves on a
journey to find each other, wife, lover, husband for life. Question is must we
suffer?
       some yes, but some less. Different situations, but some with right
information, right destination, mellow situation. Proper care is for all, not too
sweet, right date is a treat, make no mistake.

Mathew 19: 6. "So they are no longer two," but one flesh.
Make no mistake, one has to take proper care. Lover, wife, husband for life,
wrong or right Therefore, God has joined

       together, let no man separate. There is no mountain too high to climb.
Everybody can make the adjustment. It starts

in the soul, spirit and mind. And world peace

      has got to start in the East, then spread across the waters,
Inspired and guided by the Father.

                                    God, Creator,

Jesus,

                                    Jehovah

Immanent

                                    Gott, Dio, Dios,

Allah

John 7:38. Whoever believes in me
as Scripture has said, out of his heart will
flow rivers of living water.

Del Centro della vita, vienne de una grande fontana
l'amor che muove il sol e l'autra stella.

THIRD EYE BLUES SONG

Part One Good Guy

Need to tell you, third eye,
a long, song, poem bout right or wrong love. Midnight
doubts, fights over love rights. Got my third eye on and just
got off of da phone, was making to my girl. She been halfway
round da world, seeking dat two million collar mother
of pearl. Had to put it on Roam, till I gets back home.
Meanwhile I got it covered from da sky. Eye a little
nervous, blinking. Eye blinks once. Everything's Okay.
Twice she's having it her way. Paradise. Eye signals
she might not be alone. Eye a little double nervous, trouble.
Say baby might be getting serviced by a fellow dat works
at da superdome. Eye blinked twice while I was on
da phone, got me thinking all wrong. If I can't trust
my baby maybe I should just leave her alone. Hey look
at you. I is ready to get it on. Now I can see through
walls, concrete, horses, strolls cows, meat to eat wit
my third eye. Feel so good, I can fly higher dan a plane
up in da sky with my third eye glass. Don't need no molasses
with my French toast. Third eye can see from coast to coast.
My third eye can see my baby.
If she ever starts to run away from home, so I send my third eye
on missions when I get full of suspicions, I order eye,
say Eye, park by my baby's side make sure she don't
take Harry or Joe. For no scary roller coaster ride. Cause I
found out my red eye can cry. Just like my other two, specially
when I see baby being untrue.

Part Two

Long ago when I was young, I got sprung. Puppy love broke
my heart in two. Then I went into my room, cried 14 days and nights, didn't
know what to do. Eye got therapeutic, said, Son, all us three are gonna cry, cry,
cry, just please don't say goodbye. You always got eye and pie in da sky on dis
ride and we promise not to kick you to da side. So I took a trip to da moon, once
at midnight, now in darkness or daylight. I can see 360 degrees. So I drop to my
knees ask God, please bring me a true love, angelic, from above wit my third eye
open. No, no words need to be spoken. all my hoping, wishing, dreaming, finally
come true. Now I can taste apple pie, don't need no alibi wit my third eyeglasses
on. I can kick, trash, from here to Rome, put on my robe and gown, sit down on
my throne just like a true king, get on down, wear my gold, platinum, and
diamond rings, den sing to da queen of my wildest dreams. Den get up, beat 100
men in battle. King of da ring, can herd cattle. So in one of mine, trying to get
down to da real nitty, gritty wit another guy in any city, ol third eye closer, let's
water run free, till it's dry, cry, cry, disnumberd third eye, dude, CD music, You'll
last call, no alcohol.

One time my third eye went all da way to France seeking
mysterious Dame, Bella Donna. So he can be free to do the third eye dance.
Yeah, third eye can travel, moon walk, slam gavel, talk, cry, wink, blink. Third
eye looking de la tete aux pieds, faire une reve par la grace de Dieu, l'amour che
move le sol l'autre stella, le magie de cents instants. (looking from head to toe,
making a dream by God's grace, the love that moves the sun and the other star,
the magic of one hundred seconds). Den third eye not about to let Italy pass him
by. Sogno Reginetta de belleza, amore a prima vista. (love at first sight). Third
eye think, Bella, me segua pour faire le en instato d'aprresto (follow me to make
a stop in the name of God.) Den third eye tired in nome de Dio. eye, don't fall
tired. Das amera's hired. Ben round da world and found ciefeto amor. Third eye,
Yall, don't fall for Botas Mablo.

Part Three Third eye again dispels suspicion of sin!

One time my third eye went all da way to France. Seeking mysterio Bella Donna so he can be free to do his third eye dance. Yeah third eye can travel, moon walk, slam a gavel, talk, cry, wink, blink. So third eye lands in land of ladies scoping. De la tete aux pieds faire un reve,, Interpretation from head to toe, la grace de Dieu, by the grace of God. L'amor che move les stelle, l'altre . For the love that moves the moon and stars, in le magie de sens instans. In the magic of the moment. Then the third eye was not about to let Italy pass him by. Sogno riginetta de belleza amor vista, in the queen mother of beauty, love, mi segue, Belle at first sight. Third think, Bella mi segue por favor. Le in estato d'arreato in nome de Dios. You are under arrest in the name of God. Den third eye tired, dos amor hired, been round the world and found cierto amor. Third eye y'all, last call, no alcohol.

Again third eye foils suspension of sin, creates fourth eye, foil. divorce another time. I used eye as a private dick warned him not to fall for da 52n fake out or turn trick. See dis man call, sat, Mr. man wit da roving, flying third eye, I might get a job for your eye, lil spying. See I married dis Bella from France. She puts me three minutes in a trance. Every time she do her native belly dance and look me in de eye, I wake up. It be 1-3 days later, I smell traces of alligator. She tell me, it be only three minutes. My watch, calendar say it's been days I have been in a haze. So Mister third eye man, can I pay you to keep an eye on her? Follow her, listen to her cell phone, look through trash, mail. Come back in a month, indict or acquit cause bible say, Math: 9-5, for this reason a man shall leave his father and mother and be joined to his wife, and the two shall become one flesh.6. So then they are no longer two, but one flesh. Therefore what God has joined together, let no man separate, Mr. eye man says, "Sir I really don't want third eye roaming around for any month. I have my own house to watch, queen of my wildest dreams. Gotta make another eye fourth, swear him in, wipe lens. In defense of cierto amor gonna let facts even da score, whether it's a lie alibi, or you being high on loco love, mucho, mucho. Fourth eye on da job. He can be inconspicuous like painter Bob, but undercover for good, alias janitor Bob, brogan boots, overalls, painter's cap, shades in Fourth eye, ol rusty painted can, no front bumper, sign on side. "I can paint anything." So fourth eye no mission to satisfy suspension. First day eye picks up trail. Eye can already see man frozen in time. Hypnotized eye can see through da walls, man just sitting there, hands and chips in mid-air. Eye thinks, yeah something ain't fair. Den out comes Bella, eye think, lucky fella. She greets another guy. She didn't cry, just blinked once. D is guy driving a Gold Rolls, plates say, "Reverend Spike, do it right." Windows are tinted. A chauffer opens the back door. She steps in dressed in jeans and a sweat shirt, tennis shoes, black baseball cap, small duffel bag in hand. So fourth eye follows, dey go out of town to a spiritual camp ground. Sign says, River of cleansing and purifying, anointed holy water. Eye see her go into a room, "ladies only," Eye closes and looks through wall. Ten minutes and she comes out in a white gown, holding a holy book, with a crown on her head. Reverend Spike comes out on the other side, ankle length gray robe, waving hands in da air. A about 30-40 men, women, and children around reverend Spike going through a cleansing procedure, sprinkling holy water, praying, reading the scripture. Dis go on for two days and nights. Nobody eats. Eye had to have vision and man, cuisine from de snack rack in van; chips, nuts, juice jerky. Den all da men go into one place, all the ladies go into another. Den Reverend Spike drive Ms. France and six more, drop off, rest, get on bus, leave. Den me janitor for eye man come back, report goes into head eye man's office,. Den I go, "hey head eye man. Dat girl, she innocent. I just follow her two days and two nights, with night vision. She no play, no stray, no law in strange hay, but purified, sanctified." So ifn you needs me go de whole month, I can go back. But first, call Mr. suspicious man and give him da report, tell man suspicious mission abort and give him to be loco, nude cabeza, don't be a no-emo-zero, just try to please her. Den head eye man call suspicious man saying, " Sir, come look at de video, see Ms. France not starring in another's man's video, only dancing for the good Lord." Now bout your missing time suspension. It's all in your mind. "Beauty and love will send you to another dimension, just stay in Third, that's the key to claim love's rights unsuccessfully. No need for you to spend more money. Place your Honeys true to da good Lord, den self, den you. Read Mathew 6:33 Seek first the Kingdom of God and his righteousness, and all these things will be added unto you."

TRUE FRIEND

A true friend is one who'll be there
    through thick and thin. He's got your back to the very end.
He'll give you the shirt off his back under no conditions,
    introduce you to k-2 or crack. He's take your shoes
even if they didn't fit, walk 20 miles till feet screamed
    quit. They'd do all this and more, to feel your feel and let
you know that he's for real, he won't make no deals to cross
    you out. If he knows trouble's coming, he'll show you
an escape route, he won't sit at your table, eat your bread,
    watch your cable, knowing enemies want your head. If he
knew plots were forming, he'd be the first to give you
    a warning, give you time to chose wisely, so your life
you don't lose lively. He won't enter your house when
    you're not at home, knowing your wife is all alone. He's not
your typical mouse after cheese before coming. He'll call,
    on da phone. You not there, he'll change his tone, for
He's cool as a breeze and if its a she, and you're dating foe
    or friend, for you get too far in, tell you bout Joe, Rick,
or Harry. So you don't make a mistake, love and marry. Yeah
    she would break da code they all value, so we all for your
sake. If love is fake, keep you from taking a trip straight
    to hell. Yeah, she'll steer you clear of tear jerking
heartbreak, for fear you can't take feminine disguised
    as hate. Put clearly, she'll wisely advise find another date.

TIME

We like aged wine, cause it just
gets better with time. Can't drink
before its ready. Like the farmer
throwing seeds, some fell
on rocky ground, others
fell by the wayside, and others
fell on fertile ground,
sprouted right away.

TWO OLDER BROTHERS

My brothers always showed lil fish how to swim. They were both street hustlers and players. When I was eight years old, one of the houses we hung out in was owned by a very attractive lady who was called Sin. Most of the sixties groups went there; esquires, intruders. Sin was only one of oldest brother's girls. They were adults, but I was where I shouldn't have been, following my brothers. Another nickname I had was shadow. After a rotten deal being sent to Booneville, both square up and got jobs. They reached he American hood dream.

Willie, the oldest got married to a woman called Skinny. She had beautiful brown eyes, shoulder length hair. She worked as a cashier at Walkers' donut shop, which my cousin bought. Then she found another job. Willie drove a truck delivering stuffed animals. I remember how in the sixties he bragged about how he aced the chauffeurs and the regular test. He was smart. He had his own apartment. Hi would pick me up, drive me around and show me how to drive his 56 three speed. Before that he had a big Buick.

Before marrying, Sin short him in the leg. Sin's house was a party house, but she swore that she could never have another man the way she loved Willie. To prove it, she playfully pulled a 38 from her pillow. She told him with tears in her eyes, "I love you, can't let nobody else have that." Then she shot him in the leg. Neither of us lived there. Willie was just making his rounds, sex and money. When we were ready to leave she pulled that stunt. Willie would dress so well that he would stay in most ladies' dreams. They talked about him, chased him with guns, money and cars, all because they wanted to have a lil fun. Sure he'd run, have fun. He was tall, dark, had long hair, was very muscular, one bad,

loving son of a gun. It must have been his looks he always said. That's all it took

After "Sin's" sin and Boonville, Willie wanted to settle down. He wanted to

have kids with Skinny. Then he said that maybe love was just an elusive dream.

So we talked about real love, hustling, fake love. One day I asked him, When

Ms. Sin shot you, why did she tell you that she loved you, He replied, "Oh, I'm

good. They all say that." Then I asked, "Do you love all the way or just some?"

He said, "depends, some I love more than others. Now you're too young, but I

know what you see and what you do. These women are way to old, but you'll get

a good education, Use it right. Don't be on Front street."

One time, J.B. pimp, his friend, used to come over and rap, try to talk me

out of stuff. I'd make him sweat and everybody would laugh and would tell him,

"you got all dem girls and can't talk an eight year old kid out of his radio and his

money." Willie was charismatic, diplomatic, fun and easy going. Was he a

player? Naw, just a man doing manly things.

After marriage, work, church, one time the preacher pulled my mom to the

side and told her to tell Willie to stop creeping through his daughter, Joyce's

window. She was so good looking, tall, with a light complexion and golden hair.

One day I had a souped up my three speed bike. Willie asked me if he could use

it. I said, "Rent, for how long? "and He said "Gotta pay Joyce a visit while pastor

is at work. Here is one dollar. Be back in three hours." When it was getting dark,

here comes Willie, huffing and puffing on burnt rubber. He told me, "Boy, I

almost got caught. I pulled up and hit da window."

Willie and his friends would work all week. Then drink, party on the

weekends take turns driving, and switching cars. It was sleeting, freezing, and one car slid on ice, and hit the pole. It was a bad accident. Willie was killed. Freddie was injured pretty bad. Everyone in the car was hurt. Freddy, Willie's best friend died.

Sometimes I cried, specially the night Freddy died, in the early sixties. First Mike got shot twice in da stomach in our front room for skimming. He was laying on floor talking till the ambulance came. It was sort of the norm though, walking around people bleeding, some telling you who to call.

But my older brother's friends were experts who taught me everything. Two of them were the biggest players from coast to coast. They used to practice rapping wit me, for some reason, hypothetically catching fish. One of the rappers was from a line of Golden Gloves boxers. He taught us well. One of them went into the military, There was a martial arts expert, who was very proficient. He taught me about fashion. We had to dress for success, win in every contest while being clean. You had to walk away as a winner. Not only did you have to win love and war, but you had to talk more smack than Mohammed Ali while doing it. And while when is came to shooting pool, call your next two shots before you made em.

Willie's favorite songs, "Too Weak to Fight," "Hang on Sloppy," Baby, Baby don't Cry," "Tracks of my Tears." By then I was way off track. Took me years to come back, filled to the top with PTSD. It was normal though. Nothing wrong. I have to listen to positive spirit, but most folks don't wanna hear it. They say that living right and the American dream is only flying kites in movies scenes.